GROOKS
3

PIET HEIN

GROOKS
3

GENERAL PUBLISHING COMPANY LIMITED
TORONTO

With the assistance of Jens Arup

Copyright © 1970 ASPILA SA.

General Publishing Company Limited
30 Lesmill Road
DON MILLS, Ontario

First Canadian Edition

Reprinted 1971,

The collections of
GROOKS
are published by
General Publishing Co. Ltd
Ontario, Canada
Doubleday & Company, Inc.
New York, U.S.A.
Hodder and Stoughton Limited
London, England
and
BORGENS FORLAG
Copenhagen, Denmark

Over 310,000 copies of GROOKS
printed in English
62,000 copies in print in Canada

ISBN 0-7736-1004-9 (paperback)
ISBN 0-7736-0015-9 (hardcover)

Printed in Canada by
T. H. Best Printing Company Limited

GROOKS
3

THRIFT

Nobody can be lucky all the time;
so when your luck deserts you in some fashion
don't think you've been abandoned in your prime,
but rather that you're saving up your ration.

CAPACITY

A contribution to the psychology of disappointment

Some people live
    in a dream of what'll
allow them to
    live their dream:
they solemnly hold out
    a half-pint bottle
and ask for
    a pint of cream.

THAT WEARY FEELING

Do you know that weary feeling
     when your mind is strangely strangled
and your head is like a ball of wool
     that's very, very tangled;
and the tempo of your thinking
     must be lenient and mild,
as though you were explaining
     to a very little child.

3

ONE'S OWN WEATHER

You're squandering
        spleen on your brothers,
and wasting
        good self-pity too,
if you think
        that there's sun on the others
whenever it's
        raining on you.

TWO PASSIVISTS

Eradicate the optimist
who takes the easy view
that human values will persist
no matter what we do.

Annihilate the pessimist
whose ineffectual cry
is that the goal's already missed
however hard we try.

THE CENTRAL POINT

A philosophistry

I am the Universe's Centre.
No subtle sceptics can confound me;
for how can other viewpoints enter,
when all the rest is all around me?

MOUSE AND MAN

A relativistic grook on co-existence

A human being sharing with a mouse.
Each thinks himself the master of the house.
In fact, of course, each occupier's place is
the other's insulating interspaces.

THREE FACTS ABOUT TRAFFIC

Three facts, quite easy,
    should be known to all
        would-be arrivers
            who set out on wheels:

that roads are greasy,
    safety margins small,
        and fellow-drivers
            fellow imbeciles.

VITA BREVIS

A lifetime
is more
than
sufficiently long
for people
to get
what there is of it
wrong.

ETERNITY AND THE CLOCK

A homage to finity

Eternity's one of those mental blocks –
    the concept is inconceivable.
The clock concedes it in ticks and tocks,
    belittled, belaboured, believable.

Each passing moment is seized and chewed
    with argument incontestable.
Premasticated, like baby food,
    eternity is digestible.

ASTRO-GYMNASTICS

Do-it-yourself grook

Go on a starlit night,
　　stand on your head,
leave your feet dangling
　　outwards into space,
and let the starry
　　firmament you tread
be, for the moment,
　　your elected base.

Feel Earth's colossal weight
　　of ice and granite,
of molten magma,
　　water, iron, and lead;
and briefly hold
　　this strangely solid planet
balanced upon
　　your strangely solid head.

TWIN MYSTERY

To many people artists seem
    undisciplined and lawless.
Such laziness, with such great gifts,
    seems little short of crime.
One mystery is how they make
    the things they make so flawless;
another, what they're doing with
    their energy and time.

DRAWING NEAR

To Saul Steinberg

You draw
the near things
    nearer
by making
clear things
    queerer.

THOUGHTS AND THINGS

I concentrate on
   the concentric rings
produced by my pen
   in the ink.
The thing that distinguishes
   thoughts from things
is that thoughts are harder
   to think.

LAST THINGS FIRST

Solutions to problems
    are easy to find:
the problem's a great
    contribution.
What is truly an art
    is to wring from your mind
a problem to fit
    a solution.

ON BEING ONESELF

Good-resolution grook

If virtue
can't be mine alone
at least my faults
can be my own.

UNPLUMBED DEPTHS

Grook on philo-sophistical and other -isms

Philo-sophisticism
    with hypnotic
effect affects
    the boobies that abound:
being so bottomlessly
    idiotic
that even they
    can see it is profound.

ORIGINALITY

Original thought
   is a straightforward process.
It's easy enough
   when you know what to do.
You simply combine
   in appropriate doses
the blatantly false
   and the patently true.

WISDOM IS –

Wisdom is
the booby prize
given when you've been
unwise.

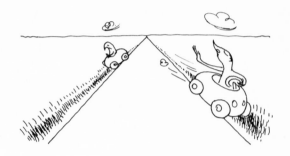

THE OPPOSITE VIEW

For many system-shoppers it's
a good-for-nothing system
that classifies as opposites
stupidity and wisdom,

because by logic-choppers it's
accepted with avidity:
stupidity's true opposite's
the opposite stupidity.

HERE IT IS

Here's good old Earth –
— what a dear little star!

Here's U.S.A. –

— here's U.S.S.R.

Washington
is over here –

— and Moscow's
over there.

What an ugly face
for such a lovely World to wear!

21

PROSPECTING THE SUMMIT

A grook about parlour games

Those who've been making the week go by
trying to work out exactly whom, with
what reservations, and how, and why,
who would (or wouldn't) remain in the room with,

ought to consider, anent their doom,
a further point they can play the goat with,
viz.: to discover exactly whom
who might (or mightn't) be in the same boat with.

UNDERTONE

One must admire the cool deliberation
with which they talk of thermonuclear power:
as if the very earth's disintegration
will also be forgotten in an hour.

BRIDGING MATERIALS

Is there a mote in your neighbour's eye?
Bridge-builder, leave it alone!
Humanity's bridges can only be built
of the beams in your own.

ONLY HOPING

Only hoping isn't what
gives us strength to cope.
Let us only hope; but not
o n l y only hope.

WANTING TO BE ABLE TO

'Impossibilities' are good
   not to attach that label to;
since, correctly understood,
if we wanted to, we would
   be able to be able to.

WHO IS LEARNED?

A definition

One who, consuming midnight oil
in studies diligent and slow,
teaches himself, with painful toil,
the things that other people know.

THE EGOCENTRICS

People are self-centred
to a nauseous degree.
They will keep on about themselves
while I'm explaining me.

EVERYBODY'S WORTH KNOWING

It's some sort of comfort
    to get the gist
of certain impertinents
    I could list –
so that you know what you
    haven't missed.

GROOK ABOUT FAITH, HOPE, ETC.

She gave me hope,
she gave me love,
    with bounty unalloyed.
But what she had of faith,
alas,
    she gave to Freud.

THE CIVILIZED ART

Two types that had far better
    leave to their betters
the civilized art
    of exchanging letters
are those who disdain
    to make any response,
and those who infallibly
    answer at once.

IN PRAISE OF ABUNDANCE

I love excess
of fruitfulness.
Let other fools
pay more for less.

THE FIRST PRINCIPLE
OF GASTRONOMY

There's a rule for proper doses
in the dinner-eater's lore:
one should stop the filling process
while one still has room for more.

And if someone at the table
had reminded me before –
Hallelujah! I'd be able
to absorb a little more.

HANDSOME IS –

Portrait-grook

He's gallantry personified;
    in fact
his brochures ought to read:
SATISFACTION GUARANTEED –
or your virginity returned
    intact.

IDLE FELLOW

Portrait-grook

Professor Blooby doesn't see the fun
in what his fellow-men call relaxation.
He isn't ignorant of how it's done,
but lacks the necessary application.

A DIPLOMATIC COMPROMISE

A fellow I know
can get mountains to move
and all opposition
appeases:
he preaches what God
cannot help but approve,
and does
what the Devil he pleases.

POLYMANIA

Clearly the Fates
were in one of their spins,
and what became me
was intended as quins.

So all my sublime
aspirations are vain,
with five of me kneading
our thoughts in my brain.

NOVELTY

For me there is something ineffably new
   in every new moment's arising;
and even the things I habitually do
   have qualities new and surprising.

There's nothing that happens that happened before
   in exactly that way in its life.
When you're playing the piano, it's rather a bore;
   but it's nice when you're kissing your wife.

REVELATION AT MIDNIGHT

Infinity's taken
      by everyone
as a figure-of-eight
      written sideways on.

But all of a sudden
      I now apprehend
that eight is infinity
      standing on end.

NUMBERS

A number will find
fulfillment enough
in knowing its mind
and doing its stuff.

INFLUENZA CLASSICA

'O Varus, Varus, give me back
my legions!'
                    Augustus Caesar.

With a head that aches severely
and with weeping nose and eye
I lie helplessly extended at full length;
and like old Augustus – nearly –
I beat my breast and cry:
'O Virus, Virus, give me back my strength!'

REMEDIES' REMEDIES

Pills are useful
against ills
and against
too many pills.

WE DO OUR BEST

Or do we?

Modern man
has the skill:
he can do
what he will.
But alas –
being man
he will do
what he can.

CHEAP EATERY

Whenever I'm scared by the state of my purse
    I dine at the 'Gold-Digger's Claim',
where the food is so out of comparison worse
    you forget that the price is the same.

GREY GIANT

Elephantasy

Felled by the storm
the beech lies humbled,
roots in the air
and leaf-crown tumbled.

Woodmen arrive
in scarves and parkas
scrambling about
the beech tree's carcass,

cutting it up,
with wild irrelevance,
into spare parts
for worn-out elephants.

45

SIMILARITY

Commutative Law

No cow's like a horse,
and no horse like a cow.
That's one similarity
anyhow.

THE PARADOX OF LIFE

Philosophical grook

A bit beyond perception's reach
I sometimes believe I see
that Life is two locked boxes, each
containing the other's key.

BUDGETING: THE FIRST LAW

If you want to know
where your money went,
you must spend it quickly
before it's spent.

AH, SUN-FLOWER! WEARY OF TIME ...

Emblem-grook

Sun-flowers are weeping; winter has begun;
and even this most sun-besotted flower,
the very emblem of midsummer sun,
takes on the likeness of my bathroom shower.

ON AN ASHTRAY

When your thirst
and hunger cease,
may your ashes
rest in peace.

OH BOTHER!

What with one thing
    and another
    people bother.

With a third thing
    and a fourth it
    isn't worth it.

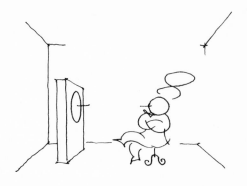

TIME

Does time exist?
I gravely doubt it.
But gosh, what should we do
without it?

CANDLE WISDOM

If you knew
what you will know
when your candle
has burnt low,
it would greatly
ease your plight
while your candle
still burns bright.

TITLE INDEX

First line index